Not a Spot to Spot

For KJ, unique as can be, like Kipekee
—E. W. V. (or Lizzie, as KJ calls me)

For Freja—keep being uniquely you
—Z. W.

SIMON & SCHUSTER BOOKS FOR YOUNG READERS • An imprint of Simon & Schuster Children's Publishing Division • 1230 Avenue of the Americas, New York, New York 10020 • © 2025 by Simon & Schuster, LLC • Book design by Tom Daly • All rights reserved, including the right of reproduction in whole or in part in any form. • SIMON & SCHUSTER BOOKS FOR YOUNG READERS and related marks are trademarks of Simon & Schuster, LLC. • For information about special discounts for bulk purchases, please contact Simon & Schuster Special Sales at 1-866-506-1949 or business@simonandschuster.com. • The Simon & Schuster Speakers Bureau can bring authors to your live event. • For more information or to book an event, contact the Simon & Schuster Speakers Bureau at 1-866-248-3049 or visit our website at www.simonspeakers.com. • The text for this book was set in Tarif. • The illustrations for this book were rendered digitally. • Manufactured in China • 0325 SCP • First Edition • 1 2 3 4 5 6 7 8 9 10 • Library of Congress Cataloging-in-Publication Data • Names: Verdick, Elizabeth Weiss, author. | Waring, Zoe, illustrator. • Title: Not a spot to spot : the true story of Kipekee, the giraffe born without spots / written by Elizabeth Weiss Verdick ; illustrated by Zoe Waring. • Description: First edition. | New York : Simon & Schuster Books for Young Readers, 2025. | "A Paula Wiseman Book." | Audience term: Children | Audience: Ages 4–8. | Audience: Grades K–1. | Summary: When a reticulated giraffe is born without spots, her differences are celebrated, and she is named Kipekee, meaning "unique" in Swahili. • Identifiers: LCCN 2024038028 (print) | LCCN 2024038029 (ebook) | ISBN 9781665962025 (hardcover) | ISBN 9781665962032 (ebook) • Subjects: CYAC: Giraffes—Fiction. | Animals—Infancy—Fiction. | Individual differences—Fiction. | LCGFT: Animal fiction. | Picture books. • Classification: LCC PZ7.1.V4615 No 2025 (print) | LCC PZ7.1.V4615 (ebook) | DDC [E]—dc23 • LC record available at https://lccn.loc.gov/2024038028 • LC ebook record available at https://lccn.loc.gov/2024038029

Not a Spot to Spot

The True Story of Kipekee, the Giraffe Born without Spots

Written by
Elizabeth Weiss Verdick

Illustrated by
Zoe Waring

A Paula Wiseman Book
Simon & Schuster Books for Young Readers
New York   Amsterdam/Antwerp   London   Toronto   Sydney   New Delhi

Summer sky . . . a hot July . . .
and something special was due.

Such a bright day at the Brights Zoo!

Mama Giraffe,
strong and sure,
stood waiting, waiting
for what would come soon.
A gift wrapped in hide . . .
her baby,
unique and one of a kind.

With a *whoosh*,
the baby giraffe, or calf,
landed on solid ground.
Hello, world!

Mama's gentle eyes and grateful nuzzles said, *Welcome*.

"Hmm," said the zookeepers as the calf dried off.
"Where are her spots?"

Mama had spots.
The zoo's other giraffes had spots.
Wild giraffes in the African savanna did too.
The spots on their hides helped the giraffes to hide.

But *this* little giraffe was all one shade.
Tawny in the bright light
and soft like summer grass.

Not a spot to spot!

With Mama's gentle kiss, the baby giraffe tried to rise. . . .

Tremble

Wobble

The calf took her place by Mama's side.

One small, one tall . . . a wondrous day for all.

"Have you heard?" murmured the giraffe herd.
"A new baby has arrived!"

Mama Giraffe just knew,
from her head to her hooves,
that her baby was
unique and one of a kind.

Perfectly herself.

On her first day outside,
the calf's eyes opened wide.

The sun!
The sky!
The warm earth on which to stand.

And the herd . . .
they all stuck their necks out
and licked the little calf.

"Welcome to your home."

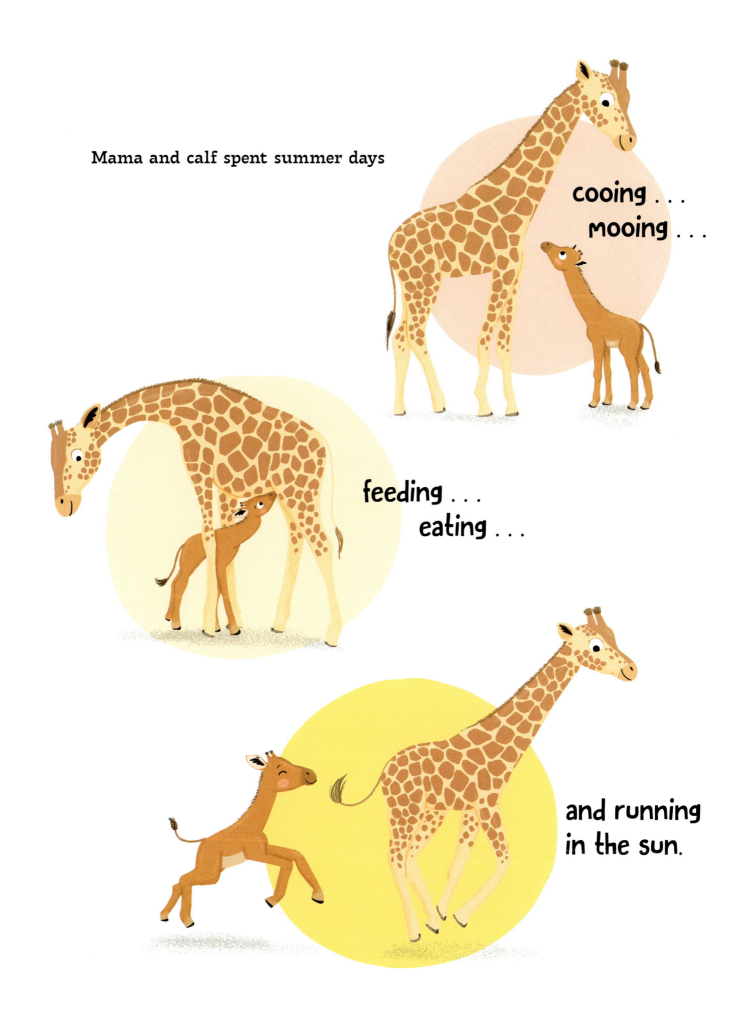

When the calf slept,
head tucked to tail,
Mama Giraffe watched over her,
whispering,
"Grow up strong and sure.
Always stand tall.
Be proud of who you are."

Word spread . . .

from mouth to mouth . . .

and across the world.

People said: "No *spots*?"

"How new! How rare!"

"What will you name her?"

"Hmm," said the zookeepers.
"A name has meaning.
We must choose well!"

They decided to ask people for help.
"A name in the Swahili language,
to honor the African heritage
of giraffes," said the zookeepers.

They waited and waited, then tallied
the votes. And the world chose . . .

Kipekee.

"Kipekee" in Swahili means "unique."

One of a kind.

Visitors came from miles and miles away.
The people oohed, and they aahed.

"Kipekee! Kipekee!"

Yes, thought Mama. *Now* they see.
She's perfectly herself—my Kipekee.

And the little calf . . . ?

There she stood, strong and sure,
bright in the spotlight,
growing taller and taller each day.

One of a kind
like you . . . like me.

Proud to be Kipekee.

More about Kipekee

Not a Spot to Spot was inspired by a special event at the private, family-owned Brights Zoo in Limestone, Tennessee. On July 31, 2023, a rare reticulated giraffe was born. The zookeepers (the Bright family) realized how unique this baby giraffe was—not since 1972 in Tokyo, Japan, had another spotless giraffe been born in captivity. After researching such an unusual event, the Brights learned that another spotless baby giraffe was seen in the wild in Africa sometime after the birth at their own facility. At Brights Zoo, the other giraffes accepted the new baby right away, not caring that she looked different. Her human family was grateful that the new no-spots giraffe was born at the zoo rather than in the wild, improving her chances of survival.

The reticulated giraffe (*Giraffa camelopardalis reticulata*) is native to the Horn of Africa and is one of the species most commonly seen in zoos around the world. Its hide typically has large brownish spots outlined in white or cream. When the new baby giraffe at Brights Zoo was born all one color, a lovely shade of tan, the zookeepers understood that she could help draw attention to the need for giraffe conservation efforts worldwide. Giraffe populations are in decline due to habitat and resource loss, as well as illegal hunting. People around the world grew more interested in giraffes once they heard about the baby born at Brights Zoo.

The Bright family wanted to give the calf a special name, one in the Swahili language. They came up with four possibilities and asked the public to vote on which name they liked best. Kipekee it was! "Kipekee" means "unique." If you go online, you can listen to the pronunciation of this Swahili word, which sounds like kee-pay-KAY. Now, at Brights Zoo, most people pronounce the name more like kip-pe-kee.

David Bright, the zoo's director, describes their charming giraffe addition as "curious" and "laid-back." This singular creature can remind us all that being different is not just okay but awesome! Each one of us is unique—or should I say, kipekee?